LIVING IN THE ZONE

KNOWLEDGE EVERY SUCCESSFUL PERSON SHOULD HAVE

DR. RONALD E. COTTLE

WITH STUDY GUIDE

Living in the Zone

KNOWLEDGE EVERY SUCCESSFUL PERSON SHOULD HAVE

Dr. Ronald E. Cottle

All rights are reserved solely by the author. The author guarantees all contents are original and do not infringe upon the legal rights of any other person or work. No part of this book may be reproduced, stored in a retrieval system, or transmitted in any form or by any means without expressed written permission of the author.

Unless otherwise noted, all Scriptures are from the King James Version of the Bible ® Copyright © 1982 by Broadman & Holman Publishers, Nashville, TN, Used by permission. All rights reserved.

Scriptures marked NKJV are from the New King James Version (NKJV) of the Bible. Copyright 1979, 1980, 1982 by Thomas Nelson, Inc. Used by permission. All rights reserved.

Scriptures marked NIV are taken from the HOLY BIBLE, NEW INTERNATIONAL VERSION. Copyright © 1973, 1978, 1984 by International Bible Society. Used by permission of Zondervan Publishing House. All rights reserved.

Scriptures marked AMP taken from the The Amplified ® Bible, Copyright © 1954, 1958, 1962, 1964, 1965, 1987 by The Lockman Foundation: La Habra, CA. Used by permission

Scriptures marked NLT are from the Holy Bible, New Living Translation copyright© 1996, 2004, 2007 by Tyndale House Foundation. Used by permission of Carol Stream, Illinois 60188. All rights reserved. Tyndale House Publishers Inc.

Scriptures marked PHILLIPS are from The New Testament in Modern English, Revised Edition, J. B. Phillips © 1980 Simon & Shuster, New York.

Copyright © 2022 by Dr. Ronald E. Cottle

Printed in the United States of America

TABLE OF CONTENTS

Introduction – Living in the Zone 1

Success Point 1 – Know Your Call and Purpose 7

Success Point 2 – Know Your Boundaries 15

Success Point 3 – Know Your Season 25

Success Point 4 – Know Your Associations 37

Success Point 5 – Know Your Strengths and Weaknesses . . 49

Success Point 6 – Know Your Passion and Conviction . . . 61

Success Point 7 – Know Your Enemy 71

Conclusion 75

Individual or Small Group Study Guide 77

*IF YOU HAVE NO PASSION
FOR YOUR VISION,
YOUR VISION
IS ONLY A GOOD IDEA.*

—J. Rowan Samson

INTRODUCTION

LIVING IN THE ZONE

Where there is no vision, [chazōn - ha-zone] the people perish: but he that keepeth the law, happy is he.
(Proverbs 29:18 – brackets added)

In the zone! What could that mean? In sports, it is that time when athletes find themselves consistently performing at their peak. In business, it is the point where profits are up, losses are down, and operations are at ultimate efficiency. In you, it is the place where you have found your sweet, satisfying success—doing what you were designed to do, pursuing your God-given purpose with passion and conviction. My desire for you is that you are able to live "in the zone." I want you to live your life successfully, even at times when you are facing seemingly insurmountable difficulties and trials.

Living like this is the result of knowledge, but not just any knowledge. You need the right kind of knowledge—knowledge driven by vision. You need knowledge that will cause you to focus on your potential and God's purpose. So, I want to give you seven vital things we all need, seven pieces of knowledge that will help insure your success. No matter what life throws your way, these should be etched in your soul and experience.

In order to have knowledge driven by vision, it is obvious you must have vision, so I want to address that first. When you have a God-given vision, it will be your greatest anchor and guide.

Why People Perish

Perish is the Hebrew word *para*. It is rendered numerous ways in different translations of the Bible, primarily because it has multiple meanings. The New International version translates this word *para*, "cast off restraint." In The Living Bible it is translated "run wild." In other words, those without vision are naked and unequipped to handle the pressures and obstacles that cross their paths. This is a parallel condition to one found in the book of Judges.

> *In those days Israel had no king; everyone did as he saw fit.* (Judges 17:6, NIV)

Perish (*para*) also means to retreat in fear due to lack of hope or focus. Since there was no king in Israel, no visionary authority existed in the nation. "Every man did what was right in his own eyes" (Judges 17:6, AMP).

The key word which unlocks this verse is eyes. People who are not driven by God-given vision tend to live according to their own eyes—their own focus. They do whatever they have determined is right for them. They look for whatever it takes to get ahead, whatever it takes to outdistance the other guy. They do whatever is necessary to cut others off and beat them. That becomes their main focus in life. It is the lifestyle of people who have no godly vision or divine purpose. They have no boundaries in the natural. But if you focus on the vision God has for you, even when you are in one of life's storms, you can have perspective and be at peace.

Look at the word vision. It means much more than eyesight. Vision gives you the ability to steer your life in the right direction. Vision protects you from being destroyed by your situation.

Having vision is different from having a vision. A vision is specific, a mental picture or projection of an event or situation. Vision, however, is different. It is a coordinating, synchronizing perspective regarding one's purpose and future. Vision points you to where you are headed, protected by the knowledge which is necessary to get you there. That comes from seven vital areas.

Having vision gives you the ability to make progress as you sharpen your focus on who you are in Christ and where you are going. Having vision from God engrafts His word, His personal *rhema*, into your being.

> *Thy word is a lamp unto my feet and a light unto my path.* (Psalm 119:105)

Thus, having vision sheds light on life's journey and thrusts you into God's purpose—your destiny, your direction. This is what God has placed you on the earth to accomplish during your life time. If you are focused on your God-given vision, even when you are in life's storms, His vision gives you peace and perspective. You can evaluate everything that comes into your life based on where God wants you to go and what God wants you to do.

> *And we know that in all things God works for the good of those who love him.* *(Romans 8:28, NIV)*

God is at work in all things for the ultimate good of those who love Him—big things, little things, good things, and bad things … all things. Knowing and believing that settles you, encourages you, and sets you "in the zone."

Vision is the Hebrew word *chazon* which means mental sight. What you see in your mind determines what you become in life. When you are living in your *chazon*, you are in the center of who you are, where you are going, and what your purpose is in God. If you can see it, you can be it. If you can say it, you can have it or do it.

That is the purpose of this book. I want you to learn how to live in your *chazon*, your vision, your zone.

> *His divine power has given us everything we need for life and godliness through our knowledge of Him who called us by His own glory and goodness.* *(2 Peter 1:3, NIV)*

There are seven key areas of knowledge we all must have if we are to live in our *chazon*. God has made them available to us through His divine power. Hosea 4:6 says, "My people are destroyed for lack of knowledge" (AMP). Knowledge you have failed to receive is knowledge you will never walk in. One of Satan's deadliest weapons against us is ignorance. Ignorance, or lack of knowledge, does not excuse us from God's purpose. But the right knowledge ensures success.

> *The heart of the prudent acquires knowledge, and the ear of the wise seeks knowledge.*   *(Proverbs 18:15, NKJV)*

Gaining the right kind of knowledge is a sensible, far-sighted thing to do. And these seven areas of knowledge provide for success. You and I will have a much more successful life by knowing these things, putting them into practice, and remaining focused on fulfilling our God-given vision.

> *Therefore, my brothers, be all the more eager to make your calling and election sure. For if you do these things, you will never fall.*   *(2 Peter 1:10, NIV)*

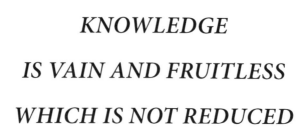

KNOWLEDGE IS VAIN AND FRUITLESS WHICH IS NOT REDUCED TO PRACTICE.

—MATTHEW HENRY

Success Point 1

Know Your Call and Purpose

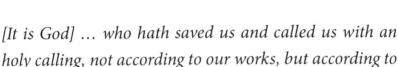

[It is God] ... who hath saved us and called us with an holy calling, not according to our works, but according to His own purpose and grace, which was given us in Christ Jesus before the world began. (2 Timothy 1:9)

In order to live in the zone, you must have knowledge of your calling and purpose in life. Jesus had a statement of purpose for His life.

For this purpose the Son of God was manifested that He might destroy the works of the devil. (1 John 3:8, NKJV)

Jesus came, much like a saboteur behind enemy lines, to untie the manacles the devil had put on human kind. That is why He came to the planet. It is His statement of purpose. He had no doubt about His mission and this anchored His success. He communicated many things as goals, but this was His statement of purpose.

As you begin your quest for success, you will need to answer three very important questions.

▶ Do you know who you are?

▶ Do you know where you are going?

▶ Do you know why you are here?

These three questions will help you in creating a purpose statement that will guide your life and ministry. Do you have a personal statement of purpose? If not, why not?

Successful people know their core purpose in God. These folks don't try to be the best at everything—a jack-of-all-trades. They have a variety of skills and can do all sorts of things. I love people like that. Usually, however, these people work for someone who has a single, clear, driving vision—someone who has a *chazōn*. So, even if you are multi-talented, lay hold of your *chazōn*. Then, specialize in that. Make your vision from God your top priority. Specialize until you become special.

SPECIALIZE UNTIL YOU BECOME SPECIAL.

The fine tuning you need to become specialized usually happens in times of turmoil—in the heat of battle or in times of crisis. You need to understand this, for these are the times you discover who you really are. This defines your direction and your destination, pointing you to your mission. This is where you are supposed to be going. Truly successful people focus on what they do best. They concentrate on their area of expertise until they become the best they can be. They specialize in the capacity God has put inside of them.

This is how you know you're in the zone—when you are working in and fulfilling the *chazōn* God has placed in you. Moreover, when you are living in the zone, you will likely have jack-of-all-trades people seeking to work for you and with you. But you will be certain about your purpose.

> *Therefore I do not run uncertainly (without definite aim).*
> *I do not box like one beating the air and striking without*
> *an adversary.   (1 Corinthians 9:26, AMP)*

The apostle Paul uses several analogies to explain why it is important to stay focused on your specific God-given mission and purpose. He speaks of running a race with a specific goal in mind and remaining focused on that goal. He describes the futility of boxing wildly, just beating the air, instead of focusing on your opponent. He also uses a military analogy to say the same thing.

> *No soldier when in service gets entangled in the enterprises*
> *of [civilian] life; his aim is to satisfy and please the one*
> *who enlisted him.   (2 Timothy 2:4, AMP)*

If you do not stay focused on what God has purposed for you, distractions will get you off track. You can chase after the wrong prize, battle the wrong enemy, and get caught up in things that have nothing to do with your purpose. The devil will put an abundance of good things to do in your path. Don't get frustrated. Just because something is good doesn't mean it is God's plan and purpose for you.

The enemy will say something like, "Look at this. Wouldn't this be nice?" He will even help you be successful in that because he knows it is outside of your zone and eventually it will destroy you. He will tell you it will make you rich, and it might. But it will take you away from your destiny, away from being the person God has designed you to be. Far too many people go to their graves without ever knowing their true purpose in God. What a tragedy that is for any child of God.

> *It is God who saved us and called us with the holy calling not according to our works but according to His own purpose and grace which was given us in Christ Jesus before the world began.* (2 Timothy 1:9, NKJV)

Through Jesus, God saved us and called us. But He did not do so because of anything we have done—our works. He did this for His own purpose, the one He had in mind for us—our destiny, even before the creation of the world. This verse is autobiographical of Paul. He understood that this was how God had dealt with his life. Verses 10 and 11 go right along with it.

> *[It is that purpose and grace] which He now has made known and fully disclosed and made real [to us] through the appearing of our Savior Christ Jesus…For this I was*

appointed as a herald (preacher) and an apostle (special messenger) and a teacher of the Gentiles.

(2 Timothy 1:10-11, AMP)

Paul knew who called him and why he was called. He knew where he was going as well. He knew he was a preacher, an apostle, and a teacher. God did not keep it a secret from him. Neither will He keep your purpose from you.

You were not an afterthought, an appendix to God's plan. Your calling and anointing were established long before you were born. They are as old as dirt, older even. Before God ever spoke the worlds into place He already knew you. Before you ever came out of the womb of your mother, God had set you apart. He knew who you were, what you were to do, and what you were going to need to do it. He put everything that you would ever need on the inside of you as seed to be developed. He wants you to live in the zone and become everything He designed you to be.

> **YOU WERE NOT AN AFTERTHOUGHT, AN APPENDIX TO GOD'S PLAN.**

Before I formed you in the womb I knew and approved of you [as My chosen instrument], and before you were born I separated and set you apart, consecrating you; [and] I appointed you as a prophet to the nations.

(Jeremiah 1:5, AMP)

If you can make God's purpose your whole and focused purpose, there is nothing that can stop you. Why? Because in Christ you can do all things—everything required to accomplish His purpose.

> *I have strength for all things in Christ Who empowers me [I am ready for anything and equal to anything through Him Who infuses inner strength into me; I am self-sufficient in Christ's sufficiency]. (Philippians 4:13, AMP)*

If what you are doing is in Christ, you are ready for anything and equal to anything. As you live in Christ, He will give you His power to fulfill His purpose for your life. That is life in the zone. More than you could ever ask or think or believe is possible for you. So, if you make God's purpose your purpose, there is a great future ahead. You need to have the knowledge of your calling and purpose in God.

Too many of us live on the outskirts of our holy city—the one God designed for us to live in. We are suburbanites, but God wants us to move into the inner city and accomplish His purpose. When we do, we become powerful, successful, productive leaders of His army.

Key Points for Living in the Zone

- In order to live in the zone, you must have the knowledge of your calling and purpose in life.
- Successful people focus on what they do best. They specialize until they become special.
- When you are living in the zone, you will have jack-of-all-trades people seeking to work for you and with you.
- If you do not stay focused on what God has purposed for you, distractions can get you off track. You will chase the wrong prize, battle the wrong enemy, and get caught up in things that have nothing to do with your special purpose in God.
- Just because something is good does not mean it is God's plan and purpose for you.
- If you can make God's purpose your purpose, there is nothing that can stop you.

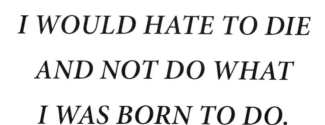

*I WOULD HATE TO DIE
AND NOT DO WHAT
I WAS BORN TO DO.*

—T.D. Jakes

Success Point 2

Know Your Boundaries

We will not boast of authority we do not have. Our goal is to stay within the boundaries of God's plan for us.
(2 Corinthians 10:13, NLT)

If you desire to live life in the zone, you must have the knowledge of your boundaries. No matter how great and powerful you are, there are boundaries to your spiritual authority. You must know the reach of your authority or else you will reach beyond God's provision.

The biblical term for measure is *metron*. It indicates the extent of the influence and authority you have from God. We do have authority (Gk. *exousia*). Although this word is usually translated power, it is not physical or political power. It is the permission to exercise power.

We only have the permission to exercise divine power within our specific sphere (*metron*) of authority and within our boundaries. No matter how great you are or how large your ministry may be, there are boundaries surrounding your spiritual authority.

The importance of one's boundaries becomes clear as you read about how King Saul exceeded his. He and the gathered company of Israel were in Gilgal, arrayed for battle against the Philistines. But they were waiting for Samuel to arrive and make sacrifice before they entered into battle.

> *Saul waited seven days, according to the set time Samuel had appointed. But Samuel had not come to Gilgal, and the people were scattering from Saul. So Saul said, "Bring me the burnt offering and the peace offer [which he was forbidden to do]." And just as he finished offering the burnt offering, behold, Samuel came! Saul went out to meet and greet him. Samuel said, "What have you done?" Saul said, "Because I saw that the people were scattering from me, and that you did not come within the days appointed, and that the Philistines were assembled at Michmash, I thought, The Philistines will come down now upon me at Gilgal, and I have not made supplication to the Lord. So I forced myself to offer a burnt offering." And Samuel said to Saul, "You have done foolishly! You have not kept the commandment of the Lord your God which He commanded you; for the Lord would have established your kingdom over Israel forever. But now your kingdom shall not continue; the Lord has sought out [David] a man after His own heart, and the Lord has*

> *commanded him to be prince and ruler over His people, because you have not kept what the Lord commanded you.* *(1 Samuel 13:8-14, AMP)*

After the dedication of the tabernacle in the wilderness—God's dwelling place in the earth, only priests were to allowed to offer sacrifices. Saul was the king. As such, he was God's anointed and appointed leader of Israel. But he was not permitted to operate in a priestly role. When he operated within the authority as king, Saul was able to achieve victory. But when he stepped outside of his sphere (*metron*) of authority, he lost his anointing as king.

> *Samuel said, "Although you were once small in your own eyes, did you not become the head of the tribes of Israel? The Lord anointed you king over Israel. And he sent you on a mission.... For rebellion is like the sin of divination, and arrogance like the evil of idolatry. Because you have rejected the word of the Lord, He has rejected you as king."* *(1 Samuel 15:17-18a, 23, NIV)*

Peter and Paul, through their New Testament epistles, show that they understood their areas of spiritual authority also. They knew their boundaries. Moreover, the apostles in Jerusalem understood that Peter had a different sphere of ministry than that of Paul, who writes:

> *They (the apostles at Jerusalem) saw that I had been entrusted with the task of preaching the gospel to the*

> *Gentiles, just as Peter had been to the Jews. For God, who was a work in the ministry of Peter as an apostle to the Jews, was also at work in my ministry to the Gentiles.*
> *(Galatians 2:7-8, NIV – parenthesis added)*

You are not everybody's apostle. You are not everyone's spiritual father. So, your goal is to stay within the boundaries of God's plan for you.

Paul explained this principle to the churches over which he had been given authority. Each of his letters to those churches was sent with the seal or stamp of his God-given authority to speak into their lives. Paul introduced his letters to the Corinthians, the Galatians, the Ephesians, and the Colossians as "Paul, called to be an apostle of Christ Jesus by the will of God."

> *After all, though you should have ten thousand teachers (guides to direct you) in Christ, yet you do not have many fathers. For I became your father in Christ Jesus through the glad tidings (the Gospel). So I urge and implore you, be imitators of me.* *(1 Corinthians 4:15-16, AMP)*

In letters to Timothy and Titus, Paul adds the salutation, "To my true son in the faith." He had even greater authority over those who were specifically his sons in the faith.

Paul knew his sphere of authority and stayed within the boundaries God had given him. By doing so he influenced a large geographic area on his missionary journeys. Thus, at the end of his life he was able to say, "I have fought the good fight, I have finished the race, I have kept the faith" (2 Timothy 4:7, NIV).

When you operate within your God assigned sphere, you have the right to exercise His power. But it is not automatic. You will have to pay a price for it with a life of holiness and commitment to purpose. When you are operating within your boundaries, you will also find that you obtain increased authority.

> **YOU WILL HAVE TO PAY A PRICE ... HOLINESS AND COMMITMENT OF PURPOSE.**

Paul is an example of a man who paid the price with a commitment to purpose. He stayed the course and even urged others to imitate his example.

Ann Coulter, a conservative political commentator and author, wrote a book entitled *Shut Up and Sing.* She was primarily addressing Barbara Streisand's penchant for speaking into the world of politics. Most people know that Ms. Streisand is one of the most talented singers on the planet. However, her rhetoric from a far left ideology is one which also reveals the fact that she is less than well informed on political matters.

By writing *Shut Up and Sing*, Ms. Coulter is basically saying, "Why don't you stay in your zone?" Perhaps some of us need the same kind of suggestion. **Live in your zone!**

You Are Great When You Are in Your Zone

Get in your zone and stay in your zone. You are great when you are in your zone. But when you get outside of it, you miss the mark and lose your focus. Boundaries are not given to hinder us. They are like the banks of a river. They keep us flowing toward our destiny. They hold us in, focus our energies, and strengthen our effectiveness. Consider the strength and power of a river flowing freely within the confines of its banks. Then look at the chaos that happens when it overflows. Floods, destroyed property, shattered lives, and significant financial loss follow. Without banks along rivers, the earth would be a swamp teeming with poisonous creatures and vicious predators.

> **BOUNDARIES ARE NOT GIVEN TO HINDER US.**

When you operate outside of your God-assigned boundaries, you become toxic as well. Boundaries are good; limitations are necessary. They are friends, not foes. This same thing is true of the anointing God has placed on our lives. What joy it is to flow freely in the anointing of God. Miracles, signs, and wonders happen regularly when we are flowing in our anointing.

Saul was a powerful king who saw many victories when he stayed within his boundaries. But when he stepped outside those boundaries, he blocked the power of God from flowing in his life. Everything went downhill from there. What a sad thing it is to see people struggling, coping, and trying to make it outside their anointings.

When you step beyond the limitations of your *chazōn*, you are really on your own. But when you live in the zone, you have the "wind beneath your wings." You have the power of God operating in your life, and there is "joy unspeakable full of glory" (1 Peter 1:8). No matter what the circumstances are that gather around you, God is with you and will work through you when you are in your zone.

> *We, on the other hand, will not boast beyond our legitimate province and proper limit, but will keep within the limits [of our commission which] God has allotted us as our measuring line and which reaches and includes even you. For we are not overstepping the limits of our province and stretching beyond our ability to reach, as though we reached not (had no legitimate mission) to you, for we were [the very first to come even as far as you with the good news (the Gospel) of Christ.*
> (2 Corinthians 10:13-14, AMP)

We should not carelessly try to move in and out of God's vision for us. We need to live in the zone. God's purpose for us should permeate our lifestyles. If we want to walk in peace in the maelstrom of life, we need to maintain our boundaries.

Jesus said of Himself:

> "My food, my nourishment, the very substance of my life is to do the will of Him who sent me and to accomplish that. It is to finish completely the work He has destined for me." (John 4:34, – author's paraphrase)

He did just that. Thus, in the throes of anguish as He hung on the cross, He could cry out in victory, "It is finished." Redemption was perfected because Jesus knew His zone and stayed within the boundaries the Father had given Him.

John 5:3 tells us there were a great number of disabled people at the pool of Bethesda when Jesus came there. They were waiting for a miracle healing, but Jesus offered a healing touch to only one of them. There were times during His walk on earth that Jesus healed everyone who came to Him. His compassion extended to everyone. However, on this occasion, God sent Him specifically to one man.

What would have happened if He had healed every person sitting or lying by the pool? Would it have disrupted His destiny? Jesus always did what pleased the Father—first and only. He lived in the zone. It is impossible to know. I do know this; Jesus always did that which pleased the Father.

You will never be fulfilled trying to operate in another man's sphere. You cannot possess another man's field or live in another man's zone. You will only find the richness of your life within your own zone. This is the *chazōn* God has destined for you. You have to make the choice.

Key Points for Living in the Zone

▶ Our goal is to stay within the boundaries of God's plan for us.

▶ No matter how great you are, there are boundaries on your authority.

▶ You do have the right to exercise power (*exousia*) if you are operating within your boundaries—your sphere of influence.

▶ Every person must know his sphere of influence and authority from God.

▶ Boundaries are like river banks; they are given to focus and strengthen us.

▶ You will never be fulfilled in another man's field or boundary.

*PERSONAL BOUNDARIES
ARE WHAT DEFINES
YOUR IDENTITY ...
THIS IS ME – THAT IS NOT ME!*

—Bill Gaultiere

SUCCESS POINT 3

KNOW YOUR SEASON

To everything there is a season, and a time for every matter or purpose under heaven. (Ecclesiastes 3:1, AMP)

To live in constant peace, you must have the knowledge of your seasons. Four different seasons come within each year: winter, spring, summer, and fall. Each lends a benefit to the environment and each is significant to the earth's stability. Not only that, the seasons are radically different depending on one's spot on the earth. Some regions experience great heat, others greater cold. Some experience little difference from season to season. Thus, the amazing variety of plants and animals that grow and live in various climates depend on the characteristics of the seasons in their particular location.

There are seasons in the spiritual realm as well. And unless you know this, you will find yourself operating with bad timing—out of season. So, let's look at three of the words in this verse in Ecclesiastes. The first is season. It is a translation of the Hebrew word *zeman*. It means an appointed or prearranged time. It is not an instant or a moment, but rather it is an extended period of time—weeks, months, perhaps even years. The annual cycle of the earth around the sun generates seasons of approximately three months each, but God assigns the seasons for His purposes.

> **GOD ASSIGNS THE SEASONS FOR HIS PURPOSES.**

In the spring, many different plants produce a beautiful array of flowers. Some will mature into fruits and nuts. Others will produce pollen which will allow bees to make honey. Others will mature into all manner of food. Spring is a time for growth and renewal, one that lasts for many weeks, not just a few days.

Next comes summer, when growing things flourish and bear fruit. Crops mature and produce food, trees spread their leafy canopies, showing off their majesty, basking in the sun and drinking in the rain. The summer season also lasts for several months: sultry times when children play and older folk tend to grow a bit lazy.

Summer gives way to fall and foliage begins to recede. Leaves drop as trees prepare for coming snow. Crops are gathered and food is stored away. The natural energy built up in the summer goes down into root systems, and plants which cannot endure the cold die back to a dormant state. Spiritually, this is the root time of life, time when strength is stored up to withstand harsh weather and to wait for the return of growth. When spring comes again, this stored energy rises to its purpose and a whole new vista of life unfolds.

Inevitably winter comes. Cold, icy, freezing wind and blinding snow cast a pall of grey over the countryside. Life slows; animals seek shelter to wait out the storms to come. There's a beauty in winter, however. Where the snow becomes deep, a pristine whiteness blankets the fields. Families draw close around the warmth of a fire and the fellowship of life takes on new meaning.

Of course, some regions of the world do not experience dramatic seasonal changes. Folks who live in these areas miss the dramatic shifts in weather. So it is with many people in their spiritual lives as well. All too often they too miss the benefit and blessing that are so apparent in the changing of the seasons.

SEASONS OF LIFE HAPPEN TOO

Whether you noticed it or not, you have gone through many seasons in your life. Unlike the repetition of the earth's annual parade, yours is not repetitive. Life for you has marched forward since you were born. First, you were an infant. Then you were a child. Eventually you entered that season when you were not really a child, but you were not really an adult either. Still, the seasons passed and life moved forward.

Before you were married, you were in one season—a time of singleness. You were carefree and unsure of the future. When you found that special someone and married your spouse, your whole life changed. You moved into a completely different season. Your spouse's interests became your interests and you had to work through many differences and desires with one another. Next came the time you held your first child. In that moment, you entered yet another season of life, one that lasts not months, or years, but decades.

I could go on, but you know where this is going. As you moved from season to season, you changed. You discovered you had different levels of responsibility, different kinds of pleasure, and pain you never imagined. You became quite a different person as you moved from season to season. From the time you were a child, you were learning that you had to go through seasons of growth in order to become a mature adult. If you didn't, you would not be able to function productively.

Every successful person looks back on his or her life and sees the importance and necessity of seasons. They have gone through quite a number of them to reach the level of success they have achieved. Someone who starts at the bottom and works his or her way up in business may eventually become a manager or a superintendent. By diligently working through each phase or level of that business, one becomes a more efficient manager than someone else is brought in from the outside. The outsider may know about the business. He doesn't know much about how it functions in that place. A person can have significant technical knowledge, but not the seasoning of experience (going through seasons of development). Without that, he may lack the wisdom or the insight to lead it successfully.

God's Season for Israel

God knew the children of Israel needed a season of preparation before they could make it in the Promised Land. In Deuteronomy 8, God reminds them of their journey through the wilderness and why they had to go through that season. This passage offers a significant explanation for us too, especially when we are going through our desert. Question God's timing if you will, but read the following passage and you will understand. God accomplishes His purpose in trying times.

> *You shall remember that the LORD your God led you all the way these forty years in the wilderness,*
>
> ▸ **to humble you and test you, to know what was in your heart, whether you would keep His commandments or not.**
>
> ▸ *So He humbled you, allowed you to hunger, and fed you with manna which you did not know nor did*

> *your fathers know,* **that He might make you know that man shall not live by bread alone; but man lives by every word that proceeds from the mouth of the LORD** *(Deuteronomy 8:2-3, NKJV, emphasis added)*

- *that He might humble you and that He might test you,* **to do you good in the end.**
  (Deuteronomy 8:16b, NKJV – emphasis and bullet points added)

Know Your Time Zone

To everything there is a season, and a time for every matter or purpose under heaven. (Ecclesiastes 3:1, AMP)

To everything there is a season. We have covered that. But then the verse states that there is a time to every purpose under heaven. Our measurements of time are a result of the earth's rotation around its axis. Every location on the earth passes the sun each day. A day and a night are divided into twenty-four segments, each segment requiring a specific amount of time to make this journey. As a result, the earth is segmented into twenty-four time zones, four of which occur in the United States: Eastern, Central, Mountain, and Pacific. Alaska and Hawaii are actually outside the time zones on the mainland, and the time throughout the remainder of the world can be very different from what your clock face shows.

Overlooking the difference between these zones can cause you to miss an important meeting, a flight, an appointment, a conference call, or some other deadline. In business, you need to know which time zone your client is in and schedule your conversations according to that difference. If you are dealing with multiple clients or members of a team, each participant must know the correct timing of a call in his or her zone as well. Failure to coordinate such communications will create chaos and a breakdown in productivity. Timing them accurately is extremely important. This is especially important in today's high tech society where so much business is conducted from remote destinations. Having a working knowledge of time differentials is crucial to your success.

The same principle holds true in the kingdom of God. Timing—being in sync with God's time zone is vital to the fulfillment of your vision. Your season (*zeman*) is His time zone (*zeman*). It is that period in which you live out the next chapter of your purpose—life's story. If you don't learn to function within God's time zones—His timing, you may do some very good things, but they will be done in the wrong season. Such timing errors can cause you to produce an Ishmael instead of an Isaac.

> God's timing is so important. At times we will have to wait on Him for either His answer or the right time to do His will. Waiting may be harder than actually doing what He wants. [2]   – Dr. Larry Keefauver

Abram, who was later renamed Abraham, received an amazing promise from God. He would have an heir from his own body even though he and his wife Sarah had never been able to have children (Note: Genesis 15:4).

A detailed story follows telling how, in the discouragement of their season, Abram and Sarai decided to help God out. Ishmael was the result. They simply decided to help God by trying to bring the fulfillment of this promise outside of God's timing. So, when Abram was eighty-six, Ishmael was born, not to Sarai, but to Hagar, a maidservant. In Genesis 16:12, the Angel of the Lord described Ishmael as "a wild donkey of a man; his hand will be against everyone and everyone's hand will be against him, and he will live in hostility toward his brothers" (NIV).

But after he was born, the voice of the Lord went silent. Genesis 16 ends with this verse.

> *And Abram was fourscore and six years old, when Hagar bare Ishmael to Abram.* (Genesis 16:16, KJV)

The next statement is verse one of Genesis chapter 17.

> *And when Abram was ninety years old and nine, the LORD appeared to Abram,* (Genesis 17:1, KJV)

For fourteen years after the birth of Ishmael the Lord did not speak to or appear to Abram. He had missed God's timing and life must have been a very silent season.

Abraham and Sarah ultimately did receive their child of promise, Isaac. However he was born in God's timing. Abraham was a hundred years old and Sarah was ninety when Isaac was born. Both were beyond what anyone would consider to be the right season or the right time for this to happen. But God brought about His purpose in His timing—God's time zone.

Learn to operate within the time zones of God. God's got them for all of us whether we are in business or ministry or education or whatever. God has certain time zones in which specific things are ordained. When we understand that, He will work with us and we will achieve success.

> **LEARN TO OPERATE WITHIN GOD'S TIME ZONES.**

In the Greek language, one word for time is *chronos*. This is time which can be measured, time which registers on a clock. It is earth time: 24 hours in a day, 7 days in a week, 52 weeks in a year. But God's timing is not simply *chronos*—earth time, it is time and timing according to His purpose and plan.

ACTIVATING GOD'S SEASON
YOUR TRIGGER TIME

But My covenant I will establish with Isaac, whom Sarah shall bear to you at this set time next year."

(Genesis 17:21, NKJV)

The word for time here is the Hebrew word *eth*, which in the Greek is translated *kairos*. It is a set time, God's time—God's now. So many preachers miss this point when they talk about a *kairos* moment in God. The word *kairos* does not actually mean being in the moment. Rather, it is a trigger for timing—the activation point for the next season.

You need to learn to read and understand the seasons and the time zones of God. You need to work with God to engage in whatever God is doing. Restrain yourself from doing what you want at the moment. Good people can be wrong. You can absolutely do the right thing, do it in the right way, and do it for the right reasons. But if your timing is wrong, you will miss God's will. Abraham did the right thing, but he did it at the wrong time and birthed Ishmael instead of Isaac. Learn to deal in the seasons and time zones of God by watching for those *kairos* trigger times from God.

God starts every time zone *zeman* with a *kairos* or an *eth*, a trigger time. You enter a new time zone immediately after a trigger point and you get called into that new place—that new season. It is a new time zone of God.

Perhaps the best way to sharpen your senses and be on the lookout for your *kairos* trigger moment is to know God's will and purpose for your life. Every successful Christian begins the journey to success by seeking to know God's purpose for his or her life. Without that purpose, you have no plumb line by which to judge your decisions and actions. If you don't know where you are going, how can you map your journey? God alone knows the paths you are to take, so it is imperative that you continually seek to know His purpose and will for your life. Then if you get off track, you will be able to return to His charted course.

The Greek word for purpose is *chephetes*. It means divine desire, pleasure, and will. We certainly do not want to miss God's will for our lives. The Bible tells us we can know His will for our lives and how to discover it.

> *I beseech you therefore, brethren, by the mercies of God, that you present your bodies a living sacrifice, holy, acceptable to God, which is your reasonable service. And do not be conformed to this world, but be transformed by the renewing of your mind, that you may prove what is that good and acceptable and perfect will of God.* (Romans 12:1-2, NKJV)

And another translation offers this:

> *"Don't copy the behavior and customs of this world, but let God transform you into a new person by changing the way you think. Then you will learn to know God's will for you, which is good and pleasing and perfect."*
> (Romans 12:2, AMP)

One of the greatest lessons I have learned is to understand this principle and do things in God's season, His timing, and His will. Ninety percent of the will of God is timing.

God has made everything beautiful for its own time.
(Ecclesiastes 3:11, NLT)

KEY POINTS FOR LIVING IN THE ZONE

▸ Every successful person looks back on his life and sees the importance and necessity of the various seasons he went through to reach the level of success he has achieved.

▸ You can do the right thing in the right way for the right reason but at the wrong time and miss God's will.

▸ 90 percent of the will of God is timing.

▸ We can learn to know God's will for our lives.

▸ God starts every new time zone with a *kairos*, a trigger time.

▸ Every successful Christian has to start on his journey by seeking to know God's purpose for his or her life.

---

[1] *Friend to Friend* copyright 1983 by J. David Stone and Larry Keefauver; TEC Publications, Columbus, GA

Success Point 4

Know Your Associations

Bad company can make those who want to live good become bad. (1 Corinthians 15:33, NLT)

People can be your greatest asset or your worst problem. They will work with you or against you, filling you up or draining you out. You simply must have the right kind of associations. During times of turmoil and challenge, wrong associations will drag you down. Look at this verse again as the Amplified Bible offers it.

Do not be so deceived and misled! Evil companionships (communion, associations) corrupt and deprave good manners and morals and character.
                                        (1 Corinthians 15:33, AMP)

Every relationship you enter will either be beneficial or detrimental to your life. It will build you up or wear you down, strengthen you or sap your energy.

As men and women who live in the zone, we must always be careful who we allow to have access to the intimate areas of our lives. God chooses our families, both natural and spiritual. That does not mean everyone will have a positive effect on us. He expects us to choose our intimate friends carefully.

Be friendly, but don't become a close friend to just anyone you meet. The people who gather around you will either encourage you or discourage you. Some folks always seem to have a dark cloud hovering over them. Hang around them for very long and they will dampen your spirit.

ENCOURAGEMENT VS. DISCOURAGEMENT

To encourage someone means to inspire them with courage and hope. Encouragers reassure you and raise your spirits so you can keep moving toward your God-given purpose. Discouragers undermine you, weaken your courage and smother your confidence. When you become discouraged, you lose the boldness to move forward toward fulfilling your destiny in God. Even well-meaning fellow Christians, when they don't have the same vision you do, can discourage you. They may tell you what you are trying to do is impossible. Don't listen! And don't draw them close to you. Tell them God gave you this vision and move on. Seek out those who will encourage you, will walk with you, and will propel you forward. Tell yourself "with man this is impossible, but not with God" because you know "all things are possible with God" (Note: Mark 10:27).

Your associations will either make you better, or they will make you bitter. Remember, hurting people hurt people. If you allow bitterness or unforgiveness to have access to your heart, you will give the enemy a foothold in your life. His goal is to keep you from fulfilling God's plan and purpose. He will send others to you who will urge you to hold onto unforgiveness or bitterness. If a so-called friend continually brings up how others hurt, disappointed, or wounded you in the past, they are not going to help you get better. They are going to point you down the path to bitterness. Good friends will remind you of God's forgiveness and love toward you. They will encourage you to forgive and love others as well.

> **YOUR ASSOCIATIONS WILL EITHER MAKE YOU BETTER OR BITTER.**

> *Get rid of all bitterness, rage, anger, harsh words, and slander, as well as all types of evil behavior. Instead be kind to each other, tenderhearted, forgiving one another, just as God through Christ has forgiven you.*
> *(Ephesians 4:31-32, NLT)*

ASSOCIATIONS AFFECT EFFECTIVENESS

Strong, encouraging relationships will make you more effective, while negative associations will do the opposite.

Close positive friendships have greater honesty than those which are superficial. Friends like these can speak to your weaknesses and limitations, yet they will speak in love, knowing the importance of your purpose. Others who do not have your interests in mind will flatter you with words while they undermine your destiny.

As iron sharpens iron, so a friend sharpens a friend.
(Proverbs 27:17, NLT)

Wisdom comes through honest interaction with a good friend who can offer a constructive critique without being critical in judgment. Proverbs 27:9 says, "The heartfelt counsel of a friend is as sweet as perfume and incense" (NLT). Your close relationships should stretch you and challenge you to become all God has called you to be.

THE COMPANY WE KEEP ALWAYS AFFECTS US.

The company we keep always affects us one way or the other. God expects us to love all people. However, He does not expect us to become a close associate with everyone. We must be wise when allowing individuals into the inner core of our lives. Who we are in Christ, where we are going in God, and His ultimate purpose for our future is at stake. To live the *chazōn* life—life in the zone—you must have clear knowledge of right associations. That means you must also be willing to disengage from relationships that are detrimental to your success as God defines it.

Two Biblical Examples

The Second book of Samuel records the tragic conflict between David and his son Absalom. This young man rose up in treason against his father. 2 Samuel 13-18 is a comprehensive record of that tragic time. In chapters 16 and 17, Absalom received advice from two men, Ahithophel the Gilonite, who has been David's counselor, and Hushai, the Archite, who was David's friend. Hushai's advice would have pointed Absalom down a path to success. Ahithophel's advice did just the opposite. But Absalom chose to follow the wrong advice, a choice which ultimately led to his destruction.

When choosing associations, especially when selecting those from whom you will receive counsel, it is crucial to make the right choice. The results will be victory or defeat, fulfillment or failure.

Another biblical narrative sets a completely opposite tone. In Acts 27:27 – 28:3-6, Paul was a prisoner on a ship bound for Rome. Aboard were 275 other men, some were sailors, some were soldiers, and some were prisoners. A severe storm blew in and after two weeks, it was clear the ship would be lost. The sailors sought to escape and the soldiers wanted to kill the prisoners and try to survive.

The wisdom of the moment would have been to abandon ship, but Paul had the word of the Lord for the situation.

The Centurion in charge of the soldiers and prisoners heeded Paul's advice. Although the ship and its entire cargo was lost to the sea, every man aboard reached land safely. Whatever Paul had done to win the confidence of that Centurion, their association served to spare their lives and those of their companions.

Eventually, Paul did reach Rome and there, as a prisoner, he wrote much of the New Testament. If he had not associated with the Roman, he would have been killed with the rest of the prisoners.

Jesus had many followers, but He carefully chose twelve men to be His immediate circle. Even then, one of them betrayed Him. But there were three who, more than the others, experienced an even greater closeness with the Lord. These three were destined for key leadership positions when the Church was eventually birthed into the world.

Jesus only took Peter, James, and John to the mountain where He was transfigured (Note: Matthew 17:1-8). When He raised the daughter of Jairus from the dead, only Peter, James, and John accompanied Him into her room—no one else (Note: Mark 5:21-43). You need to guard the door through which your associations enter your life. Guard it well; it may be the door to your destiny.

Key Points for Living in the Zone

- Every relationship you enter into is either beneficial or detrimental to your life.

- Every relationship is either going to make you better or bitter.

- Every relationship is either going to make you effective or ineffective.

- Guard your associations and guard them well.

- Be wise in allowing individuals into the inner core of who you are in God, where you are going in God, and what your ultimate purpose is in God.

ASSOCIATE WITH MEN OF GOOD QUALITY IF YOU ESTEEM YOUR OWN REPUTATION; FOR IT IS BETTER TO BE ALONE THAN IN BAD COMPANY.

—George Washington

Success Point 5

Know Your Strengths and Weaknesses

So for the sake of Christ, I am well pleased and take pleasure in infirmities, insults, hardships, persecutions, perplexities and distresses; for when I am weak [in human strength], then I am [truly] strong (able, powerful in divine strength). (2 Corinthians 12:10, AMP)

To live in peace in your *chazōn*—your vision, you must have genuine knowledge of your strengths and weaknesses.

For as in one physical body we have many parts (organs, members) and all these parts do not have the same function or use. So we, numerous as we are, are one body in Christ (the Messiah) and individually we are parts of one another [mutually dependent on one another]. Having gifts (faculties, talents, qualities) that differ according to the grace given us, let us use them: [he whose gift is] prophecy, [let him prophesy] according to the portion of his faith; [he whose gift is] practical service, let him give himself to serving; he who teaches, to his teaching; he who exhorts (encourages), to his exhortation; he who contributes, let him do it in simplicity and liberality; he who gives aid and superintends, with zeal and singleness of mind; he does acts of mercy with genuine cheerfulness and joyful eagerness.

(Romans 12:4-8, AMP)

A leader must know his strengths and weaknesses. A person in the zone knows his strengths are connected with his vision—his *chazōn*— and knows his boundaries. Regardless of what his flesh tells him or what the world says about him, he knows how far he can go.

Other people may tell you that you are the best preacher on the planet; you know that may not be true. They may say you are the best musician in the world, but you know someone who outshines you by a mile. Your true strength lies buried much more deeply within you than your talent. Perhaps you haven't dug deep enough in the quarry of your life to fully discover your strengths. Perhaps you should.

> YOUR STRENGTHS ARE CONNECTED WITH YOUR VISION.

Living in the zone, your strengths must be connected with your vision. You must also recognize that your boundaries lie outside of that, no matter what your flesh, your friends, or the world around you tells you. You gain strength by staying within your zone, and when you step outside of it, you grow weak.

You have something inside of you that belongs to the body of Christ. It is your anointing, and your anointing is always connected to your *chazōn*. What you carry about inside you is not your own. God put it in you for others, not just for you. Each of us needs all the rest of us. We are less than we could be when any of us fall short of stepping into our zone.

God has given each of us the ability to do certain things well. Some are given the ability to prophesy, others to teach. Some serve with a special flair and delight, others have a knack for encouragement. Still others have an uncanny ability to accrue finances and give them away. These are all gifts from God. They are not yours, as though they were treasure to be collected and hoarded. They are to be used to edify and encourage the body of Christ and to serve and bless God's creation. Prophesy with faith, serve with excellence, and teach with diligence. Your gift is empowered by your anointing, and your anointing is best released in your *chazōn*.

Your 3-D Strengths

Your strengths are greater than a single ability. They are three dimensional—joined to your definition, your destination, and your destiny. You are defined as who God says you are, not who or what others or the world says you are. Your destination is the place to where God is sending you, not just your job or where others say you should go. And your destiny is found within God's purpose for your life. These are the workings of God's strength in you, not simply your own physical, mental, or emotional strength.

I know I am strongest when I am functioning in my sphere of anointing. I also know I am weakest when I step out of that sphere. I teach. I lead others, especially as one who imparts wisdom through my gift. I am an apostle, called and commissioned to fulfill that responsibility within the body of Christ. I know this is what I was born to do and I am at my best when I am doing that. I also love to play golf, but I am not the world's best golfer. I see the professional golfers on television and I realize I cannot become what they are. Golfing brings me enjoyment, but it is not my zone.

People often say they were born to do one thing or another. I was born to dig deeply into the Word of God and present what I learn to as many as I can reach. When I stay in that zone, I am effective and productive in the Kingdom of God. I know who I am. I know where He is sending me, and I know what my destiny is in Him.

While David was a young shepherd, he learned early in his life not to measure his strengths and weaknesses by what others said about him. Not even his family could diminish his knowledge. While they considered him nothing more than a boy, he found his strength in his relationship with God. When the prophet Samuel came to David's father seeking to find and anoint the next king of Israel from among his sons, Jesse did not even call David to the meeting. Samuel discerned God's call on someone other than these brothers and demanded that David be summoned. Then he anointed David.

When Israel was at war with Philistia, Jesse sent David to take food to his older, stronger brothers who were serving in King Saul's army. The whole army was stymied by the mighty giant, Goliath, and David became angry. He determined to face the Philistine and everyone simply laughed in his face. But he was unmoved.

> *David said to the Philistine, "You come against me with sword and spear and javelin, but I come against you in the name of the Lord Almighty, the God of the armies of Israel, whom you have defied. This day the Lord will hand you over to me, and I'll strike you down and cut off your head. Today I will give the carcasses of the Philistine army to the birds of the air and the beasts of the earth, and the whole world will know that there is a God in Israel. All those gathered here will know that it is not by sword or spear that the Lord saves; for the battle is the Lord's, and He will give all of you into our hands."*
>
> *(1 Samuel 17:45-47, NIV)*

David knew who he was. He knew whose he was. And he knew he was where God wanted him to be. He was certain God had given him the strength to fulfill his destiny, and knew he was walking in the anointing of God and victory was assured.

This young man could not have had the physical strength to overcome the Philistine giant. Goliath was more than nine feet tall! He wore a bronze helmet and bronze armor that weighed about 125 pounds. He carried a sharp spear with an iron point that weighed fifteen pounds (Note: 1 Samuel 17:4-7). But under the anointing of God, David triumphed over the giant "with a sling and a stone; without a sword in his hand" (1 Samuel 17:50). David was in his zone!

> **UNDER THE ANOINTING ... DAVID TRIUMPHED OVER THE GIANT.**

You are stronger than you imagine you can be when you are in your zone.

The apostle Paul walked with a limp. This was not a gimpy leg, but it was a thorn in his flesh. No one knows for certain what it was. Whatever it was, it hampered Paul in his strenuous work. So he prayed to be delivered.

> *Three times I called upon the Lord and besought [Him] about this and begged that it might depart from me; but he said to me, My grace (My favor and loving- kindness and mercy) is enough for you [sufficient against any*

danger and enables you to bear the trouble manfully]; for My strength and power are made perfect (fulfilled and completed) and show themselves most effective in [your] weakness. Therefore, I will all the more gladly glory in my weakness and infirmities, that the strength and power of Christ (the Messiah) may rest (yes, may pitch a tent over and dwell) upon me! So for the sake of Christ, I am well pleased and take pleasure in infirmities, insults, hardships, persecutions, perplexities and distresses; for when I am weak [in human strength], then I am [truly] strong (able, powerful in divine strength).

(2 Corinthians 12:8-10, AMP)

When you read verse 7 of this chapter, you see that Paul already knew why God had given him this thorn. It was to defeat any potential pride that might develop because of the great revelations Paul received from God.

And to keep me from being puffed up and too much elated by the exceeding greatness (preeminence) of these revelations, there was given me a thorn (a splinter) in the flesh, a messenger of Satan, to rack and buffet and harass me, to keep me from being excessively exalted.

(2 Corinthians 12:7, AMP)

Paul's human weakness became an opportunity for the power of Christ to work in and through him. He accepted his suffering because he saw Christ's supernatural strength working through his human weakness. This man became a great apostle to the Gentiles. He journeyed on foot across much of the Roman empire as an apostle of Jesus Christ. He endured tremendous hardship, persecution, and pain. Yet, he wrote of the joy he had because of his *chazōn*.

Paul wrote much of the New Testament—doctrinal and instructional letters to churches and their leaders. This he did from various prisons. Once Paul moved into his zone, he became all that God had destined him to be. As far as we know, Paul suffered from his thorn for the rest of his life. But, in spite of that, his influence has been felt across the entire world and throughout Christian history because he became strong through the power of Christ in him.

Weaknesses Are Not All Bad

Weaknesses are not all bad. We each have areas that are simply not our strong suit. There are two reasons for this. First, they keep us human and approachable so we do not think more highly of ourselves than we ought to think. Like Paul's thorn, they keep us aware that our strength comes from the Lord.

Second, every weakness is a guidepost that says, "Don't go here!" When we know where our weaknesses are, we can easily see where we most need the power of Christ to work. In the natural, we need to understand our weaknesses and allow others to help us fulfill our purpose. As we manifest our strengths, we can help others as they work through their weaknesses. "When I am weak, then I am strong" (2 Corinthians 12:10), for then I draw strength from both Christ Jesus and His body.

I had a friend with whom I played basketball. I remember one momentous game we played. The clock was down to the last seconds of the game. All our team had to do was to steal the ball and pass it to my friend. I knew from experience where his strengths and weaknesses lay. In all our times of playing ball together, he had a success ratio of sinking a set shot from the corner only once in seven shots. So, if he shot from the corner, it wasn't going to happen. We wouldn't win. However, if he could shoot from the center of the court, his success ratio was eight out of ten. Our job was to get him positioned in the center, not the corner.

Weaknesses aren't necessarily bad. They simply say, "Don't take that shot. Take the one you're strongest in."

WHEN WEAK BECOMES STRONG

It doesn't stop there though. Often we find our greatest strengths within our weaknesses and our greatest weakness within our strengths. Let me explain. The area you have the most struggles with is usually the area in which you are most dependent on God to help you. In those areas where you are naturally strongest you depend on God's strength far less. To see God's mighty manifestation in your life and be strong in your weaknesses, you must turn your weaknesses over to God. Release them to the Lord and let Him give you His strength to be victorious in your weak areas.

This is one of the most important spiritual lessons I ever learned. For a long time, I have had a particular area of weakness in my life. Most people, other than my family, have no knowledge of it. God put me through the refiner's fire in this and I came out on the other side much stronger. I believe He uses this so I can help my spiritual sons and daughters face their weak areas. In many ways I teach out of the scar tissue that has developed over that wound.

Doctors will tell you that a broken bone, once it is properly healed, is usually stronger than it was before it was broken. Perhaps you know this from experience. Perhaps you too have had a refining fire. Believe me, we are stronger on the other side of that fire.

The refining process removes the impurities from the metal being purified. The refiner's fire also removes impurities from our lives. As we disengage from the negative influences of wrong relationships and realize our own weaknesses, we discover that God can, will, and does work in and through us much more effectively. Paul's advice to his young disciple Timothy was this:

> **THE REFINER'S FIRE REMOVES IMPURITIES FROM OUR LIVES.**

> *So whoever cleanses himself [from what is ignoble and unclean, who separates himself from contact with contaminating and corrupting influences] will [then himself] be a vessel set apart and useful for honorable and noble purposes, consecrated and profitable to the Master, fit and ready for any good work.*
>
> (2 Timothy 2:21 AMP)

And in another letter of instruction he wrote:

> *However, we possess this precious treasure [the divine Light of the Gospel] in {frail human} vessels of earth, that the grandeur and exceeding greatness of the power may be shown to be from God and not from ourselves.*
>
> (In 2 Corinthians 4:7, AMP)

The message of the Good News is like great treasure, but it is housed in fragile clay jars—our weak bodies. [2]

Key Points for Living in the Zone

- A man in the zone knows his strengths are connected with his *chazōn* and knows his boundaries no matter what his flesh or what the world tells him.

- You are stronger than you believe you can be when you are in your zone.

- Weaknesses keep us "human" and approachable so we don't think too highly of ourselves.

- Often we find our greatest strengths in our weaknesses and our greatest weakness in our strengths.

- The Refiner's fire removes impurities from our lives.

---

[2] Note on 2 Corinthians 4:7, *Holy Bible, New Living Translation, Study Bible,* Tyndale House Foundation, Carol Stream, IL, Pg. 1961

Success Point 6

Know Your Passion and Conviction

*So let those [of us] who are spiritually mature and full-grown have this mind and **hold these convictions**; and if in any respect you have a different attitude of mind, God will make that clear to you also.*

(Philippians 3:15-16, AMP – emphasis added)

God has a specific purpose for each person born on this earth. He knows what it is and what we need before we are even born. He has everything in place so we can successfully achieve that purpose, whatever it happens to be. However, if you expect to attain real success, you will be required to invest a great deal of time, energy, and determination. You will need to be properly trained and prepared, both to fill that position and to fulfill God's purpose. And that's not all. If you are truly going to live in the zone, you will need to have knowledge of your passion and your conviction.

Conviction is profound firmness in values and beliefs. These help you stay focused as you journey toward your purpose. Passion is an intensity of enthusiasm or the object of that intensity, or both. Passion unrelentingly drives you forward in accomplishing God's purpose until you fulfill your destiny. It is what the apostle Paul referred to when he determined to press on to the prize.

> *Not that I have now attained [this ideal], or have already been made perfect, but I press on to lay hold of (grasp) and make my own, that for which Christ Jesus (the Messiah) has laid hold of me and made me His own. I do not consider, brethren, that I have captured and made it my own [yet]; but one thing I do [for it is my one aspiration]: forgetting what lies behind and straining forward to what lies ahead, I press on toward the goal to win the [supreme and heavenly] prize to which God in Christ Jesus is calling us upward.*
>
> (Philippians 3:13-14, AMP)

The King James Bible states, "I press toward the mark for the prize of the high calling of God in Christ Jesus" (v. 14). Paul's passion was what he called his high calling, that indefatigable zeal which dominated his life. You too have a high calling in Christ Jesus. That must become and remain the central passion and conviction of your life. However, your high calling is not the same as Paul's. Neither is mine. Your high calling is not the same as mine, either.

You must never be content to be an echo, a mere copy of someone else's life and ministry. You are not a shadow. You are a unique individual with a profound high calling from God.

We each need to know what our specific high calling in God is and resolutely hold on to that purpose.

CREATED WITH YOUR FUTURE IN MIND

For You created my inmost being; You knit me together in my mother's womb. I praise you because I am fearfully and wonderfully made; Your works are wonderful, I know that full well. My frame was not hidden from You when I was made in the secret place, when I was woven together in the depths of the earth. Your eyes saw my unformed body; all the days ordained for me were written in Your book before one of them came to be.
(Psalm 139:13-16, NIV)

You are unique—brilliantly, remarkably put together. You are simply fabulous, even if you don't think so. God only built one of you; then He broke the mold.

Why trade in your individuality to become a copy of someone—anyone else? Your uniqueness is the container of your greatness. You must not settle for less than you were meant to be. You are a diamond, a precious jewel God created for His glory. Dig deep into the mine that is the real you and there discover the magnificent diamond God has made. When you content yourself to simply copy, mimic, or pretend to be like someone else, you give that all away.

> *Don't copy the behavior and customs of this world, but let God transform you into a new person by changing the way you think. Then you will learn to know God's will for you, which is good and pleasing and perfect.*
> (Romans 12:2, NLT)

J. B. Phillips rendered this verse in a profound word picture.

> *Don't let the world around you squeeze you into its own mold, but let God re-mold your minds from within, so that you may prove in practice that the plan of God for you is good, meets all His demands and moves towards the goal of true maturity.* (Romans 12:2, PHILLIPS)

DON'T COMPARE YOURSELF WITH OTHERS. In other words, don't compare yourself with others. When you do, your conclusion will be skewed, either by an underrated opinion of yourself, or one that is loftier than God intended you to carry. The real truth lies in what God says about you. He is the only one you need to please in this life. His plan for your life is the mold into which you fit best. So, look to what you were created to be.

> *But let every person carefully scrutinize and examine and test his own conduct and his own work. He can then*

> *have the personal satisfaction and joy of doing something commendable [in itself alone] without [resorting to] boastful comparison with his neighbor.*
> *(Galatians 6:4, AMP)*
>
> *When they measure themselves by themselves and compare themselves with themselves, they are not wise.*
> *(2 Corinthians 10:12, NIV)*

As long as you define your purpose through comparisons with others, you will never embrace a pure sense of passion for God's purpose. You need to know your own personal passion, your high calling from God, and lean into it. It is the driving force of your *chazon*.

THE PASSION OF THE CHRIST

The final hours of Jesus' life have long been described as the Passion. Numerous movies have been made portraying the agonizing death of Christ. The most difficult to watch was made in 2004 and titled *The Passion of the Christ*. The most intense suffering of Jesus' ministry is called His passion, yet He lived with unreserved conviction and determination throughout His life. Why? I believe it is because the fulfillment of His purpose lay in His death and resurrection. Throughout His ministry, that was always before His face.

Isaiah 59:17 tells how the Lord came, intent on achieving victory over the evil that was infesting God's people.

> *He put on righteousness as his body armor and placed the helmet of salvation on His head. He clothed himself with a robe of vengeance and **Godly fury.***
>
> (NLT – emphasis added)

Jesus had to have passion. He had to reach toward His high calling. It was necessary in order to complete His mission and redeem the lost children of God. The passion Jesus carried in order to complete His mission helped Him look away from everything that distracted Him. He abstained from everything that hindered Him from attaining what God sent Him to accomplish. We need that kind of passion as well. It will compel us to remain true to the path God has called us to walk.

The enemy will place a wide array of distractions along the path to your destiny in God—distractions that can cause you to become double-minded. Focusing on your passion will keep you focused on Jesus and God's will for your life.

In the letter of James, we are encouraged to read of the rewards connected to steadfastly remaining focused on God's will for our lives. We are also warned of the consequences of being double-minded.

> *Consider it wholly joyful, my brethren, whenever you are enveloped in or encounter trials of any sort or fall into various temptations. Be assured and understand that the trial and proving of your faith bring out endurance and*

steadfastness and patience. But let endurance and steadfastness and patience have full play and do a thorough work, so that you may be [people] perfectly and fully developed [with no defects], lacking in nothing. If any of you is deficient in wisdom, let him ask of the giving God [Who gives] to everyone liberally and ungrudgingly, without reproaching or faultfinding, and it will be given him. Only it must be in faith that he asks with no wavering (no hesitating, no doubting). For the one who wavers (hesitates, doubts) is like the billowing surge out at sea that is blown hither and thither and tossed by the wind.

For truly, let not such a person imagine that he will receive anything [he asks for] from the Lord, [For being as he is] a man of two minds (hesitating, dubious, irresolute), [he is] unstable and unreliable and uncertain about everything [he thinks, feels, decides]. (James 1:2-8, AMP)

The standard of our defense against the attacks and distractions of the enemy is spiritual armor—the whole armor of God.

Put on all of God's armor so that you will be able to stand firm against all the strategies of the devil.
(Ephesians 6:11, NLT)
Stand your ground, putting on the belt of truth and the body armor of God's righteousness.
(Ephesians 6:14, NLT)

Stand therefore [hold your ground].

(Ephesians 6:14a, AMP)

Standing your ground without having real passion for the task would be a nearly impossible responsibility. A powerful, determined enemy would be a formidable force to contend with. So to stand, you must profoundly want to. And to stand, you must believe—truly believe you are able to. Conviction is the belief that you can and you must; passion reinforces your convictions to the point of victory.

HOLD THESE CONVICTIONS

*So let those [of us] who are spiritually mature and full-grown have this mind and **hold these convictions**; and if in any respect you have a different attitude of mind, God will make that clear to you also. Only let us **hold true** to what we have already attained and walk and order our lives by that.*

(Philippians 3:15-16, AMP – emphasis added)

In other words, do not only be a person with passion, be a person of conviction as well. A conviction must be a principle you are determined to hold on to no matter what anyone else says or does.

*So let us **seize and hold fast and retain without wavering** the hope we cherish and confess and our acknowledgement of it, for He Who promised is reliable (sure) and faithful to His word.   (Hebrews 10:23 AMP – emphasis added)*

Never compromise your convictions. Stand on the truth of God's Word. If you never decide to stand for what is right, you are bound to fall for what is wrong. So you must develop unqualified assurance and absolute confidence in God's promises. He has promised to be with you and guide you to where He designed and equipped you to go. Live at the highest level of your *chazon*.

NEVER COMPROMISE YOUR CONVICTIONS.

> *Let us all come forward and draw near with true (honest and sincere) hearts in **unqualified assurance and absolute conviction** engendered by faith (**by that leaning of the entire human personality on God in absolute trust and confidence in His power, wisdom, and goodness**), having our hearts sprinkled and purified from a guilty (evil) conscience and our bodies cleansed with pure water.* (Hebrews 10:22, AMP – emphasis added)

Paul obviously knew how difficult it would be for us to stand firm in our convictions and pursue our passion. Throughout his letters, he used his own experiences as examples of the challenge leaders must face. He gave advice and encouraged others to stand firm in their passion and convictions just as he had done again and again.

> *For that [Gospel] I am suffering affliction and even wearing chains like a criminal. But the Word of God is not chained or imprisoned! Therefore I [am ready to]*

> *persevere and **stand my ground** with patience **and endure everything** for the sake of the elect [God's chosen], so that they too may obtain [the] salvation which is in Christ Jesus, with [the reward of] eternal glory. **The saying is sure and worthy of confidence**: If we have died with Him, we shall also live with Him. If we endure, we shall also reign with Him. If we deny and disown and reject Him, He will also deny and disown and reject us.*
>
> *(2 Timothy 2:9-12 AMP – emphasis added)*

*For whatever was thus written in former days was written for our instruction, that by [our steadfast and patient] endurance and the encouragement [drawn] from the Scriptures **we might hold fast** to and cherish hope.*

(Romans 15:4, AMP – emphasis added)

[We pray] that you may be invigorated and strengthened with all power according to the might of His glory, [to exercise] every kind of endurance and patience (perseverance and forbearance) with joy.

(Colossians 1:11, AMP)

Many people compromise their convictions in order to be popular. Compromise means they concede to something derogatory or prejudicial. They give up something in order to be accepted, either socially or in their place of employment. They are political, and they are always looking for the middle road. I call them "wet finger saints." They wet their fingers to feel which way the wind is blowing and go with that. They are gray area people who sacrifice character for acceptance, compromising their spiritual integrity in order to satisfy their need for recognition.

> *Take [with me] your share of the hardships and suffering [which you are called to endure] as a good (first-class) soldier of Christ Jesus. No soldier when in service gets entangled in the enterprises of [civilian] life; his aim is to satisfy and please the one who enlisted him.*
> *(2 Timothy 2:3-4, AMP)*

Good Things vs. God Things

All too often the wrong that catches us is good, but not best. There are things we get involved in that have nothing to do with our primary mission for God. If we are not careful, these can become entanglements which derail our primary purpose. We need to strive to please the One who enlisted us.

There are so many good causes vying for attention, so many ministries and functions you can work and serve in. You might be tempted to say yes to every opportunity, but you must not. Knowing your God-given passion and conviction gives you the strength to say no when you are really tempted to say yes. Any ministry or function not in line with God's purpose can become an entanglement. Before making another commitment, ask yourself a question. Is this a God thing, or is it just a good thing I am considering becoming involved in? If you cannot answer with certainty that it is a God thing, thank the person who sought you out for asking, but graciously and firmly decline the invitation. You have a higher calling.

Successful people are people of passion and conviction. They know who they are. They know Whose they are. And they know what God has called them to do. They are determined to fulfill the destiny God has placed within them with passion and conviction.

Key Points for Living in the Zone

- Your uniqueness is the container of your greatness. Don't settle for less than you can be.
- If you never decide to stand for what is right, you are bound to fall for what is wrong.
- Never compromise your convictions.
- Ask yourself before saying yes to another commitment, Is this a God thing, or is it just a good thing I am considering becoming involved in?

SUCCESS POINT 7

KNOW YOUR ENEMY

To this end also did I write, that I might know the proof of you, whether ye be obedient in all things ... lest Satan should get an advantage of us: for we are not ignorant of his devices.   *(2 Corinthians 2:9, 11)*

This piece of knowledge is so very important but is easily pushed aside. Satan works overtime trying not to be noticed. It is one of his subtle schemes to take advantage of God's ministers. Thus, a person living in the zone—the *chazōn*— must have knowledge of his enemy.

The New International Version renders verse 11 like this ... "in order that Satan might not outwit us. For we are not unaware of his schemes."

I saw something in this verse that helped me become successful. It was the necessity of knowing my enemy. The successful person will always have knowledge of his enemy: his enemy's weapons, his enemy's schemes, his enemies strategies, and his enemies tactics. In this verse, devices or schemes is the translation of the Greek word *noema*. This is actually a word for mind. In other words, we must not be ignorant of how Satan thinks, for his mind is filled with strategies planned for our defeat.

> *For we are not fighting against flesh-and-blood enemies, but against evil rulers and authorities of the unseen world, against mighty powers in this dark world, and against evil spirits in the heavenly places.*
>
> (Ephesians 4:27, NLT)

Many scripture passages give us insight into the way the enemy thinks and acts, as well as the weapons he deploys against us. Wisdom dictates that we should study our enemy so we can be prepared to withstand his attacks, even though they are devious.

> *Be well balanced (temperate, sober of mind), be vigilant and cautious at all times; for that enemy of yours, the devil, roams around like a lion roaring [in fierce hunger], seeking someone to seize upon and devour.*
>
> (1 Peter 5:8, AMP)

> *Put on God's whole armor [the armor of a heavy-armed soldier which God supplies], that you may be able successfully to stand up against [all] the strategies and the deceits of the devil.* (Ephesians 6:11, AMP)

The devil comes to steal. He is not here to give you anything. He will promise you everything, but giving is not his style. The only thing he gives is trouble!

The thief cometh not, but for to steal, and to kill, and to destroy: I am come that they might have life, and that they might have it more abundantly.   *(John 10:10)*

Satan desires to rob you of what God has given you. He wants to kill you, not necessarily in a physical sense, but he wants to kill every ounce of decency inside of you. He seeks to destroy you, to chop you up and leave you a bloody mess. But you must know his mind. You must know how he thinks. Never make any deals with the devil, even unsuspecting ones. You will always lose.

NEVER MAKE DEALS WITH THE DEVIL!

HIS NAMES REVEAL HIS NATURE

Take some time to research from the Bible the names attached to your enemy. This will let you know who you are up against and what he is about. Don't be content to read across this list—study the context in which these names are revealed.

He is called the devil (Matthew 4:1), Satan (John 13:27), our enemy (Matthew 13:39), and Beelzebub (Matthew 10:25; 12:24-27). In Revelation he is called the dragon (20:2) and the slanderer (12:10). In Genesis he is called the serpent (3:1-15); and again by Paul (1 Corinthians 11:3). And Jesus identified him as a murderer, a liar, and called him the father of lies (John 8:44). Your enemy is a very, very bad character indeed.

His names also reveal his strategies and the variety of ways he approaches us. But we must not be deceived by his devices—his schemes. The Bible gives us insight into how to be prepared so we can deal with the enemy and his deceptions.

> *For though we walk (live) in the flesh,* **we are not carrying on our warfare according to the flesh and using mere human weapons.** *For the weapons of our warfare are not physical [weapons of flesh and blood], but they are mighty before God for the overthrow and destruction of strongholds, [Inasmuch as we] refute arguments and theories and reasonings and every proud and lofty thing that sets itself up against the [true] knowledge of God; and* **we lead every thought and purpose away captive into the obedience of Christ** *(the Messiah, the Anointed One).   (2 Corinthians 10:3-5 AMP – emphasis added)*
>
> *So be subject to God. Resist the devil [stand firm against him], and he will flee from you. (James 4:7 AMP)*

We are not called to fight Satan in our human strength. Our weapons are mighty through God. Thus, we have confidence that we are well able to withstand the enemy's attacks. God has given us everything we need to be successful, to do whatever He has called us to do, and to be who He has created us to be. In fact, God is 100 percent for our success.

Knowing your enemy is your assurance that you can be aware of his efforts. He is determined to steal, to kill, and to destroy all that God has given you. But you have the mind [*nous*—same root word as *noema*] of Christ. (Note: 1 Corinthians 2:16)

Show him who you are. Use your authority. Show him whose you are. You belong to Jesus Christ. And show him that you know God has your back! Stand fast in your calling. Satan will have to flee.

KEY POINTS FOR LIVING IN THE ZONE

- The successful person will always have knowledge of his enemy, his enemy's weapons, and his enemy's schemes or strategies.

- Wisdom says we should study our enemy so we can be prepared to withstand his attacks even though they are often very subtle.

- We know Satan's mind. We know the way he thinks. Don't make any deal with the devil, you will always lose.

*THE DEVIL
IS A BETTER THEOLOGIAN
THAN ANY OF US
AND IS A DEVIL STILL.*

—A.W. Tozer

Conclusion

To live in the zone and be successful in the calling and purpose of God, you must have these seven kinds of knowledge.

- ▸ Knowledge of your call and purpose.
- ▸ Knowledge of your boundaries and limitations.
- ▸ Knowledge of your seasons and God's timing.
- ▸ Knowledge of your associations and relationships.
- ▸ Knowledge of your strengths and weaknesses.
- ▸ Knowledge of your passion and conviction.
- ▸ Knowledge of your enemy.

So, setting yourself up for success requires you to become well-informed. These seven kinds of knowledge set you up to live in the zone. These seven will have amazing influence on your success in fulfilling your purpose and walking in your calling. Implant these deep in the soil of your being. They will give you the confidence and tenacity you need to be successful in everything God has called you to be and do while you are on this earth. Never yield to the temptation to short circuit your journey by going around this knowledge. Those who do so inevitably fall short of fully achieving their destiny in God.

My prayer is that God will imprint this knowledge on your heart so that you will be successful in accomplishing the vision and purpose He has imparted to you by His Holy Spirit. **Live in the zone!**

Individual or Small Group Study Guide

Introduction: Living in the Zone

Proverbs 29:18 says, "Where there is no _____ the people _____."

Perish means:

- Cast off _____
- People run _____
- Retreat in fear due to lack of _____ or _____

  People are naked and _____

Vision means _____ _____.

What you see in your _____ determines what you _____ in your life.

A person's vision is his greatest _____ and _____.

Hosea 4:6 says, "My people are destroyed for lack of _____."

One of Satan's deadliest tools against us is _____.

If you focus in on the vision God has for you, then when you are in the eye of life's storm, it gives you _____ and _____.

Success Point 1
Know Your Call and Purpose

In order to live in the zone you must have a knowledge of your _____ and _____ in life.

You need to be able to answer these very important questions:

▸ Do you know your statement of purpose?

▸ Do you know who you are?

▸ Do you know where you are going?

▸ Do you know why you are here?

What was Jesus' purpose—His mission statement as declared in 1 John 3:8?

_____

_____

Successful people do not try to be the _____ at _____.

Successful people focus on what they do _____ and _____ until they are _____.

If you do not stay focused on what God has purposed for you, _____ can get you off track, get you _____ after the wrong prize, _____ the wrong enemy, and caught up in things that have _____ to do with your special purpose in God.

According to 2 Timothy 1:9:

It is _____ who saved us and called us.

But He did not save us or call us according ____ _____.

He saved us and called us for His own _____.

He had this purpose for us in mind _____ the world began.

Just because something is good does not mean it is God's _____ and _____ for you.

If you can make God's _____ your _____, there is _____ that can stop you.

Success Point 2
Know Your Boundaries

Our _____ is to stay _____ the boundaries of God's plan for us.

No matter how great you are, there are _____ on your authority.

Every person must know his _____ of influence and authority from God.

Boundaries are not given to _____ us, but like the banks of a river they are given to _____ and _____ us!

What a joy it is to flow freely in our _____; what a _____ thing to see another out of His anointing.

You will never be _____ in another man's field or boundary.

In my anointing I am a mighty, rushing river of _____ and _____.

Out of my anointing I am a slow, creeping, _____ _____!

You now need to be able to answer these very important questions:

▸ Do you know the boundaries of your influence?

- Do you know the boundaries of your authority?
- Are you operating within your anointing?
- How do you know if you are outside your boundaries?
- Are there any changes you need to make in your life to make sure you stay within the boundaries God has set in place for you?

Success Point 3
Know Your Season

To everything there is a _____ and a _____ for every _____ under heaven.

Define:

▶ Season _____

▶ Time _____

▶ Purpose _____

You can do the absolutely right thing in the right way for the right reason but in the wrong time and miss _____ _____.

Abraham did the right thing at the wrong time and birthed an _____ instead of an _____.

_____ percent of the will of God is _____.

God starts every time zone with a *kairos*, a _____ time.

Every successful person has to start on their journey to success by seeking to know God's _____ for his or her life.

You need to be able to answer these very important

questions:

- Do you know the season you are in?
- Do you know the time zone you are in?
- Are you trying to do good things instead of God things?
- Are you watching for those trigger moments?
- Have you experienced any trigger moments just before you entered a new season in your life? Explain.

Success Point 4
Know Your Associations

Bad people can make those who want to live good
_____ _____.

As Christians, we must always be careful _____ we allow into the intimate areas of our lives!

Why is this true? _____
_____

God chooses our families but He expects us to _____ our friends _____.

The _____ we keep will affect us one way or the other.

The successful person has a clear knowledge of the importance of _____ _____.

God expects us to love all people, but to be wise in allowing individuals into the inner core of who we are in God, where we are going in God, and what our ultimate purpose is in God. To accomplish this, you need to be able to answer these very important questions:

▶ Have you experienced a relationship that turned out to be detrimental to you? Explain.

▶ Have you experienced a relationship that made you

bitter instead of better? Explain.

- Have you experienced a relationship that has made you less effective instead of more effective? Explain.

- Is there a relationship in your life right now that God is telling you is not healthy for you if you want to live in the zone? Explain.

- What are you going to do about it?

Success Point 5
Know Your Strengths and Weaknesses

A person's strengths are connected to his or her
_____ and _____.

I am strongest when in my sphere of _____.

I am _____ out of that sphere.

Weaknesses are not all _____.

Weaknesses keep us _____ which means
_____.

Weaknesses are _____ saying, "Don't
_____ _____!"

Often we find our greatest _____ in our
_____ and our greatest _____ in our
_____.

The area you have the most struggles in is usually the area where you are _____ _____ on God.

The area you are strong in usually is the area you are the _____ _____ on God.

If you are going to see God's mighty manifestations in your life, you must be strong in _____ strength and not in _____.

You need to be able to answer these very important questions:

- Do you know your strengths?
- Do you know your weaknesses?
- Do you know your anointing?
- What are the areas you struggle in the most?

Success Point 6
Know Your Passion and Conviction

Paul's passion was what he called his _____ _____.

What does this mean in your life? _____ _____

No one should ever be content to be a _____, an _____, or the _____ of someone else.

You are _____.

You are _____ and _____ made.

Your uniqueness is the container for your _____.

Philippians 3:15-16 says, "So let those of us who are spiritually mature and full-grown have this _____ and hold these _____."

A successful person must have both _____ and _____.

Some people _____ their convictions in order to be popular.

Define a gray area Christian: _____ _____

Define a politically correct Christian: _____
_____

If you never decide to _____ for what is _____, you are bound to _____ for what is _____.

You need to be able to answer these very important questions:

▶ What is your passion?

▶ How strong are your convictions?

▶ Do you know a gray area Christian?

▶ Do you know how to stand firm in your convictions?

Success Point 7
Know Your Enemy

The successful person always has knowledge of his
_____.

A successful person is not ignorant of the enemy's
_____.

What does this mean? _____
_____

What does John 10:10 say the enemy's mission is?
_____, _____, and
_____.

You need to be able to answer these very important questions:

- ▶ Do I know my enemy?
- ▶ Do I know my enemy's devices and schemes?
- ▶ Do I know how to stand against this enemy?
- ▶ Do I know what to do to make this enemy flee from me?

Conclusion

Review the seven kinds of knowledge you need to be a successful person.

Write a brief description of each one.

Go back and list one thing you need to do under each of these areas to make sure you have this knowledge.

1. Knowledge of your _____ and _____.

Description:_____

_____

I need to: _____

_____

2. Knowledge of your _____.

Description:_____

_____

I need to: _____

_____

3. Knowledge of your _____.

Description:_____

_____

I need to: _____

_____

4. Knowledge of your _____.

Description:_____

_____

I need to: _____

_____

5. Knowledge of your _____ and
_____.

Description:_____

_____

I need to: _____

_____

6. Knowledge of your _____ and _____.

Description:_____

_____

I need to: _____

_____

7. Knowledge of your _____.

Description:_____

_____

I need to: _____

_____

ABOUT THE AUTHOR

Dr. Ronald E. Cottle has been serving the body of Christ for more than six decades. He has extensive experience in teaching, pastoring, public speaking, education administration and both radio and television.

He has developed more than one hundred advanced courses of Christian development and biblical training and has authored more than one hundred books encompassing ministry, leadership, biblical studies, and church development.

Dr. Cottle's teaching style has been called "scholarship on fire" by those who have attended his lectures. His unique style always contains the compassion of a shepherd, the urgency of a prophet and the wisdom of a statesman.

His thoughts and counsel are straightforward, dynamic, and powerful. His teachings will help today's spiritual leaders and other sincere "thinking Christians" to discover the mystery and the majesty of the Bible.

Dr. Cottle has earned a Bachelor of Arts (A.B.) degree from Florida Southern College, Lakeland, Florida; a Master of Divinity (M.Div.) from Lutheran Theological Seminary, Columbia, South Carolina; and a Doctor of Philosophy (Ph.D.) in Religion from the University of Southern California, Los Angeles. He also earned a Master of Science in Education (M.S.Ed.) and a Doctor of Education (Ed.D.) from U.S.C.

For more information about Dr. Ron Cottle and his numerous books and teachings, go to: www.roncottle.com.

THE COTTLE LIBRARY

Dr. Cottle has worked tirelessly in his home office for the past two decades compiling his five hundred notebooks, fifty plus college courses, fifty plus books, hundreds of sermon outlines, publications, articles, and newsletters. Dr. Cottle and Dr. Thomas Hale are cataloging everything into an online library.

The library contains digital files (PDF and Microsoft Word) available for download, streaming audio files and streaming video files.

Please visit the library at: www.cottlelibrary.com.

Made in the USA
Middletown, DE
27 October 2022

13604028R00057